Joy to the World

24 festive treats from around the world

SILKE MARTIN

PHOTOGRAPHY BY FRAUKE ANTHOLZ

Hardie Grant

BOOKS

Contents

Preface

Christmas time is baking time. Be it cookies, gingerbread or crescents, when people's houses smell of vanilla, cinnamon, nutmeg and aniseed, when marzipan, nuts and chocolate are on every shopping list, and when the old recipe books are dug out, children's eyes light up and both young and old look forward to these delicious treats. Whether in Sweden or South Africa, the USA or Italy, England or Spain . . .

Every country has its very own traditional recipes, which have been passed on from generation to generation for centuries. For example, mantecados in Spain, Christmas cookies and gingerbread in Scandinavia, nut crescents in Hungary and spicy chocolate Basler brunsli cookies in Switzerland. Every year the traditional delicacies are baked at home during Advent and are offered by bakeries and cafés, so everyone knows it's not long until Christmas.

Christmas cookies and biscuits were originally created to celebrate the birth of Christ. The very finest baked goods were prepared in His honour using delicious, carefully selected ingredients, to make a feast for the senses. And so it has remained to this very day. Many of the recipes in this book are only made during Advent, and are therefore something really special to be looked forward to all year. For every day of Advent, we have sought out a typical national recipe that will take you on a culinary journey to Italy, Ireland, Turkey, Denmark and elsewhere. Let's get started on a sweet trip around the world of Christmas bakery goodies!

Have fun dreaming and baking!

Silke Martin

ADVENT SUNDAY

INGREDIENTS

250 g (9 oz) dark chocolate · 250 g (9 oz) soft butter + a little extra · 250 g (9 oz/2½ cups) walnuts · 7 eggs · 1 tsp vanilla extract · a pinch of salt · 450 g (1 lb) caster (superfine) sugar · 325 g (11 oz/2⅔ cups) plain (all-purpose) flour · ½ tsp baking powder · 3 tbsp gingerbread spice mix · 75 ml (2½ fl oz/5 tbsp) milk · icing (confectioner's) sugar, for sprinkling

GINGERBREAD BROWNIES

Preheat the oven to 175°C (340°F/gas 3). Coarsely chop the chocolate. Then, over a low heat, slowly melt the chocolate with the butter in a small saucepan, whilst stirring continuously. Once it has fully melted, remove the saucepan from the hob. Dry-fry the nuts in a pan, then remove and coarsely chop them.

Whisk the eggs, vanilla extract, salt and sugar using a hand mixer with a whisk attachment. Blend the chocolate buttercream into the egg mixture. Mix in the flour, baking powder and gingerbread spice mix, gradually blending in the milk. Then fold in the nuts.

Line the baking tray with baking parchment. Evenly distribute the dough over it and bake for 30–35 minutes. Remove from the oven and leave to cool on a cooling rack.

Cut a star-shaped stencil from a piece of paper (about 3 cm/1 in in diameter). Cut the cake into 45–50 brownies. Then, using the stencil, sprinkle an icing-sugar star onto each piece.

 MAKES 45–50

USA

INGREDIENTS

200 g (7 oz) soft butter · 175 g (6 oz/¾ cup) caster (superfine) sugar · ¼ tsp vanilla extract · 350 g (12 oz/2¾ cups) plain (all-purpose) flour · 1 tsp baking powder

DREAM COOKIES

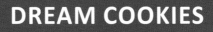

Preheat the oven to 175°C (340°F/gas 3). Lightly brown the butter in a pan (not allowing it to become too dark!) then leave to cool. Next, beat the melted butter with the sugar and vanilla extract until it becomes fluffy. Mix the flour and baking powder together in a separate bowl, then sieve into the butter mixture. Carefully combine the mixtures until it becomes a smooth, elastic dough.

Divide the finished dough into three pieces and shape into even logs, then divide each log into twenty equal-sized pieces. Roll each piece into a ball and place on a baking (cookie) sheet lined with baking parchment. Bake the cookies for about 15 minutes. Remove from the tray and leave to cool.

If you wish to decorate the dream cookies, place a blanched almond on each ball before baking.

 MAKES ABOUT 60

SPAIN

INGREDIENTS

350 g (12 oz/2¾ cups) plain (all-purpose) flour + a little extra · 125 g (4 oz/1¼ cups) ground almonds ·175 g (6 oz) lard · 250 g (9 oz/scant 1¼ cups) caster (superfine) sugar · 2 tsp ground cinnamon

MANTECADOS

Pour the flour into a pan and heat up over a low heat, constantly stirring with a wooden spoon. In another pan briefly toast the almonds, then mix with the flour and leave to cool.

Preheat the oven to 150°C (300°F/gas 1). Put the lard into a large bowl and stir until soft and creamy. Add the sugar and cinnamon. Stir again until well combined. Then gradually add the flour and almonds, and knead everything into a dough.

On a floured work surface roll out the dough to a thickness of about 2 cm (¾ in) and cut into 4 x 4 cm (1½ x 1½ in) pieces. Place on a baking (cookie) sheet lined with baking parchment and bake for 20–25 minutes. As soon as the mantecados have turned brown, remove from the oven and leave to cool.

In Spain, mantecados are traditionally wrapped separately in brightly coloured tissue paper.

MAKES ABOUT 30

INGREDIENTS

2 eggs · 250 g (9 oz) soft butter · ½ tsp ground cinnamon · 1 tsp vanilla extract · 130 g (4½ oz/ generous ½ cup) caster (superfine) sugar · 300 g (10½ oz/scant 2½ cups) plain (all-purpose) flour + a little extra · 130 g (4½ oz/generous ½ cup) cornflour (cornstarch) · 1 tsp baking powder · 40 marzipan potatoes or 150 g (5 oz) marzipan · 1 tbsp cocoa powder

CHRISTMAS KURABIYE

Preheat the oven to 175°C (340°F/gas 3). Thoroughly blend the eggs with the butter, cinnamon, vanilla extract and sugar using a hand mixer with a whisk attachment. Mix the flour with the cornflour and baking powder. Then pour it into the egg and butter mixture, carefully mix everything together and, when it comes together, knead into a dough with floured hands.

If not using marzipan potatoes, then roll the marzipan into 40 balls. Pull walnut-sized portions from the dough, flatten slightly in the palm of your hand and put a marzipan potato or ball in the middle of each one. Shape into round balls and place on a baking (cookie) sheet lined with baking parchment.

Put the cocoa powder on a flat plate, dip a suitable small cookie cutter into it, then press onto the balls to create a pattern on top. Bake the balls for about 20–25 minutes, remove from the oven and leave to cool.

 MAKES ABOUT 40

TURKEY

SWITZERLAND

INGREDIENTS

350 g (12 oz/scant 3½ cups) ground almonds · 50 g (2 oz/scant ½ cup) plain (all-purpose) flour · 1 tsp cocoa powder · a pinch of ground cinnamon · a pinch of ground cloves · 150 g (5 oz/ ⅔ cup) caster (superfine) sugar + a little extra · 4 egg whites · a pinch of salt · 120 g (4 oz) dark chocolate · 1½ tbsp kirsch, to taste sugar · brown sugar, for sprinkling

SPICY CHOCOLATE BASLER BRUNSLI COOKIES

Mix the ground almonds, flour, cocoa powder, cinnamon, cloves and sugar together. In a separate bowl, whisk the egg whites with the salt until stiff, and stir into the dry ingredients. Melt the chocolate using a bain-marie, stir in the kirsch, then add to the mixture and knead into a loose dough with your hands.

Thoroughly sprinkle the work surface with sugar and roll out the dough to a thickness of about 5 mm (¼ in) with a rolling pin coated in sugar. Then cut out various shapes, and coat each one in the sugar. Place the cookies on a baking (cookie) sheet lined with baking parchment. Leave to dry at room temperature for at least 12 hours, preferably overnight.

Preheat the oven to 175°C (340°F/gas 3). Bake the Brunsli cookies for 10–12 minutes, remove from the oven, dab on a little water, sprinkle with brown sugar and leave to cool.

MAKES ABOUT 60–70

INGREDIENTS

100 g (3½ oz) dark chocolate · 200 g (7 oz/scant 1¾ cups) plain (all-purpose) flour + a little extra · 1 tsp baking powder · 60 g (2 oz/½ cup) cornflour (cornstarch) · 100 g (3½ oz/scant ½ cup) caster (superfine) sugar · 1 tsp vanilla extract · 1 egg · zest of 1 orange · 125 g (4 oz) butter · 100 g (3½ oz) whole-milk couverture chocolate or milk-chocolate cake glaze · 1 tsp orange liqueur

ORANGE & CHOCOLATE CRESCENTS

Finely chop the chocolate. Mix the flour in a bowl with the baking powder, cornflour, sugar and vanilla. Make a whole in the middle of the mixture and put the egg and orange zest into it. Chop the butter into small pieces and place them around around the edges. Distribute the chopped chocolate over it and mix everything well using a dough hook, working from the middle outwards. Then transfer the mixture to a floured work surface and knead into a smooth dough with your hands. Leave to cool for about 30 minutes.

Preheat the oven to 175°C (340°F/gas 3). First shape the dough into thin rolls (about 2 cm/¾ in) using your hands, then divide into pieces 6 cm (2 in) long. Shape into crescents and place on baking (cookie) sheets lined with baking parchment. Bake in the oven for 15–17 minutes, then leave to cool. Melt the chocolate or cake glaze using a bain-marie, add the orange liqueur and stir well. Coat the ends of the crescents with a pastry brush, then leave to dry on a cooling rack.

MAKES ABOUT 60

19

2.

SECOND SUNDAY OF ADVENT

SOUTH AFRICA

INGREDIENTS

250 g (9 oz/2 cups) plain (all-purpose) flour + a little extra · ½ tsp bicarbonate of soda (baking soda) · ½ tsp baking powder · 1 tsp ground cinnamon · ½ tsp ground ginger · ½ tsp ground nutmeg · ¼ tsp ground cloves · 200 g (7 oz/scant 1¼ cups) brown sugar · 200 g (7 oz/1⅓ cups) chopped almonds · 120 g (4 oz) cold butter · 2 eggs · 60 ml (2 fl oz/ ¼ cup) port (or sherry) · 1 egg white

SOETKOEKIES

In a large bowl, blend the flour with the bicarbonate of soda, baking powder, spices, brown sugar and 120 g (4 oz) of the chopped almonds. Chop the butter into pieces. Whisk the eggs. Add the eggs to the flour and almond mixture together with the butter and port, mix everything together well and knead into a ball. Leave briefly to cool.

Preheat the oven to 180°C (350°F/gas 4). Roll the dough out to a thickness of about 5 mm (¼ in) on a lightly floured work surface and cut out circles (about 5 cm/2 in in diameter) with a round cutter or a glass. Place the soetkoekies amply spaced out on a baking (cookie) sheet lined with baking parchment, coat with the beaten egg white and sprinkle the remaining almonds over them. Bake for 12–15 minutes, until they have turned golden brown.

As it is easy to cut shapes from this dough you can also use other cutters, such as round ones with a wavy edge or sun-, moon- and star-shaped ones.

 MAKES ABOUT 60

INGREDIENTS

250 g (9 oz/2 cups) plain (all-purpose) flour · 125 g (4 oz) cold butter · 140 g (5 oz) dried cherries · 225 g (8 oz/scant 1¾ cups) raisins · 110 g (3½ oz/generous ¾ cup) sultanas · 65 g (2½ oz) candied lemon peel · 65 g (2½ oz) candied orange peel · 65 g (2½ oz/scant ½ cup) chopped almonds · 150 g (5 oz/¾ cup) brown sugar · zest of ½ lemon · a pinch of salt · 1 tsp instant coffee · 1 tsp gingerbread spice mix · 140 ml (5 fl oz/scant ⅔ cup) porter · ½ tsp baking powder · 2 eggs

PORTER BISCUITS

Sieve the flour into a large bowl and distribute the butter over it in flakes. Next, very finely chop 65 g (2½ oz) of the dried cherries, all the raisins and sultanas as well as the candied lemon and orange peel, and put them in the bowl together the almonds. Add the sugar, lemon zest, salt, instant coffee and gingerbread spice mix, then carefully mix everything using using a mixer with a dough-hook attachment.

Gently heat the porter in a saucepan over a low heat and dissolve the baking powder in it. Take the saucepan from the hob, then add the eggs and stir well. Add the beer and egg mixture to the flour mixture, and knead it all into an elastic dough.

Preheat the oven to 160°C (320°F/gas 2). Line two baking (cookie) sheets with baking parchment and distribute small mounds of dough on them – the best way is using two teaspoons. Don't put them too close together, as the biscuits will spread out. Finally, distribute the remaining cherries over the biscuits and bake them for 20–25 minutes.

 MAKES ABOUT 100

ITALY

INGREDIENTS

250 g (9 oz/2 cups) plain (all-purpose) flour · 25 g (¾ oz/scant ¼ cup) cocoa powder · 1 tsp baking powder · 2 tsp gingerbread spice mix · 120 g (4 oz/⅔ cup) brown sugar · a dash of vanilla extract · a pinch of salt · 30 g (1 oz) butter · 2 eggs · 1 orange · 1 lemon · 75 g (2½ oz/ ½ cup) pistachios · 75 g (2½ oz/½ cup) blanched almonds · caster (superfine) sugar, for dusting

CHRISTMAS CANTUCCINI

Knead the flour, cocoa powder, baking powder, gingerbread spice mix, sugar, vanilla, salt, butter and eggs into a smooth dough. Zest the orange and lemon, coarsely chop the pistachios and almonds, then knead everything into the dough. Wrap the dough in cling film (plastic wrap) and leave to cool for 1 hour. Then divide into four equal-sized pieces, shape into rolls about 30 cm (12 in) long and leave in a cool place for a further 30 minutes.

Preheat the oven to 180°C (350°F/gas 4). Place the rolls of dough amply spaced out on a baking (cookie) sheet lined with baking parchment, and bake in a hot oven for about 15 minutes. Leave to cool on the baking sheet, then with a serrated knife cut them into slices at an angle and bake for a further 8–10 minutes. Leave the baked cantuccini to cool on a cooling rack, and dust with caster sugar.

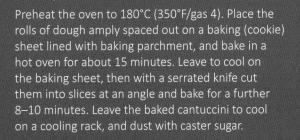

MAKES ABOUT 50

INGREDIENTS

375 g (13 oz/generous 1 cup) golden syrup or corn syrup · 50 g (2 oz/¼ cup) brown sugar · 100 g (3½ oz) butter · 500 g (1 lb 2 oz/4 cups) plain (all-purpose) flour · 2 tsp gingerbread spice mix · 1 tsp baking powder · 80 g (3 oz/⅓ cup) caster (superfine) sugar · 3 tbsp lemon juice

GINGERBREAD

Put the syrup, sugar and butter into a saucepan and heat until the sugar has dissolved, stirring constantly. Leave the mixture to cool. Mix the flour, gingerbread spice mix and baking powder. Add the cooled syrup mixture and knead everything into a smooth dough. Leave the dough in a cool place for at least 4 hours, preferably overnight.

Preheat the oven to 180°C (350°F/gas 4). Roll out the cooled dough to a thickness of 2–3 mm (⅛ in) and cut out gingerbread shapes using various cutters. Place on baking (cookie) sheets lined with baking parchment and bake for 8–10 minutes. The ginger-bread biscuits should not be allowed to go brown around the edges. Remove the biscuits and leave to cool on a cooling rack.

For the decoration, stir the caster sugar with a little lemon juice until smooth and spoon into a freezer bag. Cut off a small corner to make a piping bag, and decorate the gingerbread biscuits as required.

MAKES ABOUT 80

FRANCE

INGREDIENTS

150 g (5 oz/⅔ cup) caster (superfine) sugar + 5 tbsp extra · 100 g (3½ oz/1 cup) ground almonds + 2 tbsp extra · 2 large pinches of baking powder · 3 tsp ground cinnamon + 1 good pinch extra · 2 egg whites · a pinch of salt · 100 g (3½ oz) soft butter

CINNAMON MACAROONS

Preheat the oven to 150°C (300°F/gas 1). Finely grind the caster sugar, almonds and baking powder in a mixer or using a food processor, then pass through a sieve. Add a generous pinch of cinnamon. Beat the egg whites with the salt until stiff, then blend in 3 tablespoons of caster sugar and continue beating until the mixture is glossy and thick. Carefully blend the almond mixture into the beaten egg whites. Fill the mixture into a piping bag with a round nozzle.

Pipe 60 small mounds (about 2.5 cm/1 in in diameter) onto a baking (cookie) sheet lined with baking parchment, leaving ample space between the mounds. Press peaks flat with a wettened finger. Bake the macaroons for about 15 minutes, then leave until completely cool.

Meanwhile, stir the butter for the filling until small peaks form, mix in 2 tablespoons each of almonds and caster sugar as well as the cinnamon, then put the buttercream into a piping bag with a round nozzle. Pipe the filling between two macaroons and carefully press together, then repeat with the remaining macaroons. Leave in a cool place for at least 1 hour.

 MAKES ABOUT 30

250 g (9 oz/2¼ cups) ground hazelnuts · 2 tbsp caster (superfine) sugar + a little extra · 1 tbsp cocoa powder · 250 g (9 oz) soft butter · 250 g (9 oz/generous 1 cup) icing (confectioner's) sugar + extra for dusting · 300 g (10½ oz/scant 2½ cups) plain (all-purpose) flour · 2 tbsp cream

HAZELNUT COOKIES

Dry-fry the nuts in a pan and leave to cool. Mix the caster sugar and cocoa powder together. Cream the butter and icing sugar, then add the nuts, flour and cream and knead in well.

Shape the dough into even-sized rolls (about 3 cm/ 1¼ in in diameter) and roll them in the cocoa mixture. Wrap the dough rolls in cling film (plastic wrap) and leave in a cool place for about 1 hour.

Preheat the oven to 160°C (320°F/gas 2). Cut the rolls into slices 5 mm (¼ in) thick, place on baking (cookie) sheets lined with baking parchment and bake for about 10 minutes. Remove from the oven and dust with a little icing sugar.

 MAKES ABOUT 100

DENMARK

3.

THIRD SUNDAY OF ADVENT

RUSSIA

INGREDIENTS

200 g (7 oz) full-fat cream cheese · 200 g (7 oz) soft butter · 150 g (5 oz/scant 1¼ cups) plain (all-purpose) flour + a little extra · 50 g (2 oz/scant ¼ cup) caster (superfine) sugar · 400 g 14 oz/4 cups) walnuts · 1 egg · 75 g (2½ oz/scant ¼ cup) honey

KOLACHKI

Mix the cream cheese with the butter. Add the flour and sugar, and knead everything into a smooth dough. Leave in a cool place for 2 hours.

Preheat the oven to 200°C (400°F/gas 6). Finely grind 50 g (2 oz) of the walnuts in a mixer or using a food processor, and finely chop the remainder. Then mix all the walnuts with the egg and the honey, possibly adding a little water if the mixture is still not elastic enough.

Halve the dough and thinly roll out each half on a floured work surface. Cut 15 squares from each half of the dough. Place some filling on each square, and fold over two opposite corners so they meet in the middle. Place the kolachki on a baking (cookie) sheet lined with baking parchment and bake for about 12 minutes, until light brown.

MAKES ABOUT 30

GERMANY

INGREDIENTS

125 g (4 oz) marzipan · 3 tbsp instant coffee + 1 tsp extra · 3 egg whites · a pinch of salt ·
75 g (2½ oz/scant ¼ cup) caster (superfine) sugar · 300 g 75 g (2½ oz/scant ¼ cup) ground
almonds + a little extra · ½ tsp ground cinnamon · 1 tsp cocoa powder

MOCHA & CINNAMON STARS

Coarsely grate (shred) the marzipan. Dissolve the coffee
in a tablespoon of hot water. Beat the egg whites with
the salt and sugar for 4–5 minutes until they are very stiff
and glossy. Put 125 g (4 oz) of the egg whites in a cool
place. Add the marzipan, almonds, coffee and cinnamon
to the remainder of the egg whites and work into a
smooth dough. Wrap in cling film (plastic wrap) and leave
in a cool place for at least 2 hours. If the mixture is then
still too soft, blend in more almonds.

Mix 1 teaspoon of coffee with ½ teaspoon of water
and the cocoa powder. Take 1 tablespoon of the set-aside
egg whites, and stir in the coffee and cocoa mix. Spoon
into a piping bag. Preheat the oven to 170°C (340°F/
gas 3). Take the cinnamon-star mixture out of the
fridge and roll it out to a thickness of about 1 cm (½ in)
between two layers of baking parchment. Cut out stars
using a star-shaped cutter dipped in water. Generously
coat with the egg whites and place on baking (cookie)
sheets lined with baking parchment. Pipe the dark
egg-white mix over them in strips and, using a wooden
stick dipped in water, run the dark strips into the white
coating. Bake the filled baking sheets one after another
on the bottom rack of the oven for about 12 minutes,
then leave the on sheets to cool.

MAKES ABOUT 35

INGREDIENTS

125 g (4 oz/1 cup) plain (all-purpose) flour · 6 eggs · 125 g (4 oz) soft butter · 80 g (3 oz/⅓ cup) caster (superfine) sugar · 125 g (4 oz) dark couverture chocolate (min. 70%) · 100 g (3½ oz/½ cup) brown sugar · a pinch of salt · 125 g (4 oz) white couverture chocolate · 150 g (5 oz) apricot jam · a generous shot of rum (optional) · 300 g (10½ oz) dark couverture chocolate or dark chocolate cake glaze, for coating

SACHER CUBES

Preheat the oven to 170°C (340°F/gas 3). Sieve the flour and separate the eggs. Beat the butter and caster sugar until fluffy, and gradually add the egg yolks. Melt the dark chocolate using a bain-marie and, making sure it is not too hot, blend it into the butter and yolk mixture. Whisk the egg whites with the sugar and salt until stiff, then alternately blend the whites and the flour into the chocolate mix. Spread the dough onto a baking (cookie) sheet lined on a baking tray lined with baking parchment and bake for 30–40 minutes. Remove from the oven and leave to cool.

For the snow crystals, melt the white chocolate using the bain-marie. Draw snow crystals on to baking parchment, then turn it over. Spoon the chocolate into a piping bag, pipe snow crystals onto the prepared baking parchment and leave to dry in the fridge.

Slice the baked dough horizontally into three equal-sized pieces. Stir the jam with the rum or a little warm water until smooth. Coat the top of each of the pieces with the jam, then place them carefully on top of each other. Cut into cubes with a long, sharp knife. Melt the dark chocolate using the bain-marie. Coat the tops of the cubes with the melted chocolate. Press the snow crystals onto the still-warm chocolate. Leave on a cooling rack to drip and cool.

 MAKES ABOUT 30

AUSTRIA

INGREDIENTS

2 eggs · 120 g (4 oz) soft butter · a pinch of salt · 100 g (3½ oz/scant ½ cup) caster (superfine) sugar · 220 g (8 oz/generous 1¾ cup) plain (all-purpose) flour + a little extra · ½ tsp baking powder · ½ tsp ground cinnamon

DANISH CHRISTMAS COOKIES

Separate the eggs. Beat the butter, salt, egg yolks and 80 g (3 oz/⅓ cup) of the sugar until creamy. Mix together the flour and baking powder, sieve onto the egg and sugar mixture and knead into a smooth dough. On a floured work surface, shape two equal-sized rolls from the dough, each about 16 cm (6 in) long. Wrap in cling film (plastic wrap) and leave in a cool place for at least 2 hours.

Preheat the oven to 200°C (400°F/gas 6). Cut the rolls into slices about 1 cm (½ in) thick, slightly flatten the slices, then place them on baking (cookie) sheets lined with baking parchment. Lightly whisk the egg whites and coat the dough slices with the beaten whites. Mix the remaining sugar with the cinnamon and sprinkle it over.

Bake the filled baking sheets one after another in the oven for 10–12 minutes. Pull the cookies from the baking sheets on the baking parchment, and leave to cool.

These Christmas cookies look particularly attractive if you use sanding sugar instead of granulated sugar.

 MAKES ABOUT 32

INGREDIENTS

225 g (8 oz) soft butter · 225 g (8 oz/1¼ cups) brown sugar · 2 tbsp maple syrup or golden syrup or corn syrup · 300 g (10½ oz/generous 2⅓ cups) soft or coarse oat flakes · additional ingredients, to taste (e.g. raisins · chocolate drops · nuts · sesame seeds)

FLAPJACKS

Preheat the oven to 170°C (340°F/gas 3). Cut the butter into cubes and put in a saucepan with the sugar. Heat over a low–medium heat whilst stirring, until the butter has melted and the sugar has dissolved. Blend in the syrup and oat flakes and any additional ingredients to taste.

Fill mixture into a rectangular baking tin (about 26 × 26 cm/10 x 10 in) lined with baking parchment, and spread out evenly. Bake for about 30 minutes.

Remove the baking tin from the oven — even if the mixture is not yet firm, as cooling will make it firm enough to cut. Then cut into mouth-sized cubes or slightly bigger bars.

Your creativity should be given free rein – you can mix in dried or fresh fruit, coat the flapjacks with chocolate and/or include Christmas spices in the dough.

MAKES ABOUT 30–40

INGREDIENTS

200 g (7 oz/scant 1⅔ cups) plain (all-purpose) flour + a little extra · 175 g (6 oz) soft butter · 150 g (5 oz/⅔ cup) caster (superfine) sugar · 25 g (1 oz/scant ¼ cup) brown sugar · a dash of vanilla extract · 400 ml (14 oz) sweetened condensed milk · 200 g (7 oz) milk couverture chocolate or milk chocolate cake glaze

MILLIONAIRE'S SHORTBREAD

Preheat the oven to 170°C (340°F/gas 3). Mix the flour with 150 g (5 oz) of the butter, then add half of the sugar and knead into a firm dough. Roll out the dough on a floured work surface to form a rectangle, and put in a large tin (about 23 x 30 cm/9 x 12 in) lined with baking parchment. Prick generously with a fork and bake for about 35 minutes, until golden brown. Remove from the oven and leave to cool.

Heat the remaining butter in a saucepan with the brown sugar and the remaining caster sugar. Add the vanilla and the condensed milk and slowly bring to the boil, stirring constantly. After 3–4 minutes the mixture should have gone a caramel-like colour. Pour it over the cooled shortbread and distribute evenly. Put in the fridge for about 1 hour, until the caramel has become firm.

Melt the chocolate using a bain-marie and pour it over the caramel. Put in the fridge until the chocolate is firm. Cut into small rectangles with a sharp knife previously dipped in hot water.

 MAKES ABOUT 30

WE
WISH YOU A
MERRY
CHRISTMAS

Glad Tidings

SCOTLAND

FOURTH SUNDAY OF ADVENT

AUSTRIA

INGREDIENTS

4 eggs · 200 g (7 oz) caster (superfine) sugar · 1 tsp vanilla extract · 150 g (5 oz/1¼ cups) plain (all-purpose) flour · aniseed or fennel seeds, for sprinkling

ANISEED CURLS

Preheat the oven to 160°C (320°F/gas 2) and line a baking (cookie) sheet with baking parchment. Whisk the eggs until fluffy using a hand mixer, and gradually blend in the sugar and vanilla extract. Now beat until the mixture is creamy. Sieve the flour over it and carefully blend in.

Put small mounds on the baking sheet using two teaspoons, making sure there is enough distance between the mounds as they will spread out during baking. Sprinkle each mound with a little aniseed. Bake in a hot oven for 7–8 minutes. Remove the dough flakes from the oven and immediately curl them over a rolling pin or glass. Leave to cool and store in a dry place.

The dough flakes must be curled immediately after baking, because as soon as they get cold they will break.

MAKES ABOUT 30

INGREDIENTS

150 g (5 oz/1 cup) blanched almonds · 150 g (5 oz/1½ cups) walnuts · 150 g (5 oz/generous 1 cup) hazelnuts · 300 g (10½ oz/1⅔ cups) mixed candied fruits · 2 tsp ground cinnamon · ½ tsp ground coriander · ½ tsp ground nutmeg · ½ tsp ground mace · 75 g (2½ oz/generous ½ cup) plain (all-purpose) flour · 200 g (7 oz) acacia honey · 200 g (7 oz/generous ⅔ cup) caster (superfine) sugar + extra for dusting · 3 rectangular edible wafer papers (12 × 20 cm/5 x 8 in)

TUSCAN CHRISTMAS SLICES

In a pan, dry-fry the almonds and then the walnuts and hazelnuts until golden yellow. Leave to cool, remove the skins as far as possible and coarsely chop. Cut the candied fruits into small cubes. Thoroughly mix the almonds, walnuts and hazelnuts with the fruit cubes, spices and flour.

Put the honey in a saucepan, add the caster sugar and simmer for 2 minutes, whilst stirring. Remove from the hob, leave to cool a little, then blend with the fruit and flour to form a smooth mixture. Set aside to cool.

Preheat the oven to 160°C (320°F/gas 2). Line three baking (cookie) sheets with baking parchment. Arrange a wafer paper onto the top of each one, then evenly spread with the honey and fruit mixture, making sure not to break the paper. Bake for about 25 minutes. Pull the baked blocks and attached paper off the baking sheets. Cut each block into 10 rectangles whilst still warm, and leave to cool.

 MAKES ABOUT 30

ITALY

INGREDIENTS

60 g (2 oz) candied ginger · 250 g (9 oz) honey · 200 g (7 oz) cooked chestnuts · 120 g (4 oz/1¼ cups) walnuts · 380 g (13 oz/3 cups) plain (all-purpose) flour + a little extra · 2 tsp baking powder · 1 egg · 60 g (2 oz) soft butter · 70 g (2 oz/scant ⅓ cup) caster (superfine) sugar · a pinch of salt · 1 tsp vanilla extract · 1 tsp ground nutmeg · ¼ tsp ground cinnamon · 1 egg white · 40 walnut halves

WALNUT & CHESTNUT PRINTEN GINGERBREAD

Finely chop the ginger. Briefly heat the honey, mix in the ginger and leave to cool. Finely chop the chestnuts. Finely grind the walnuts in a mixer or using a food processor.

Mix the flour and baking powder in a bowl. Add the egg, butter, sugar, salt, vanilla, nutmeg, cinnamon, chestnuts and ground walnuts. Using a mixer with a dough-hook attachment, knead into a smooth dough, adding the gingery honey. If the dough is still too soft, add a little more flour. Wrap in cling film (plastic wrap) and leave in a cool place for about 12 hours, preferably overnight.

Preheat the oven to 180°C (350°F/gas 4). Divide the dough into four pieces and roll out each of them to a thickness of 5 mm (¼ in) on a floured work surface. Cut into 5 x 3 cm (2 x 1¼ in) rectangles and place on three baking (cookie) sheets lined with baking parchment. Whisk the egg white and thinly coat the gingerbread. Halve the walnuts and gently press in, then bake in the oven on the second rack for about 12 minutes. Leave to cool.

MAKES ABOUT 80

INGREDIENTS

180 g (6½ oz/1½ cups) plain (all-purpose) flour · 1½ tsp baking powder · 100 g (3½ oz) mint-flavoured chocolate · 150 g (5 oz) dark chocolate · 120 g (4 oz) soft butter · 100 g (3½ oz/ scant ½ cup) caster (superfine) sugar + extra for dusting · 1 tsp vanilla extract · 2 eggs

CHOCOLATE & MINT SNOW-TOPPED COOKIES

Mix the flour and baking powder in a bowl. Using a bain-marie, melt the mint chocolate and 100 g (3½ oz) of the dark chocolate. Finely chop the remaining dark chocolate. Cream the butter, sugar and vanilla. Blend in the melted chocolate and add the eggs one at a time, whilst continuing to beat. Gradually sieve the flour and baking powder mixture over it. Finally, blend in the chopped chocolate. The dough should now have the consistency of a sponge mixture, and should drop slowly from a spoon.

Divide the dough into two portions, spread each portion onto cling film (plastic wrap) to form a rectangle, wrap the cling film over and put in the freezer for about 1 hour.

Preheat the oven to 180°C (350°F/gas 4). Sieve a little sugar into a small bowl. Cut the dough into small cubes, then work with a small quantity at a time, putting the remainder in a cool place again. Shape a small ball from each cube and roll in sugar, then place the balls on two baking (cookie) sheets lined with baking parchment. Bake for 10–12 minutes, until the surface of the balls crack.

MAKES ABOUT 60

HUNGARY

INGREDIENTS

60 ml (2 fl oz/¼ cup) milk · 20 g (¾ oz/1½ tbsp) fresh yeast · 2 tbsp caster (superfine) sugar · 250 g (9 oz/2 cups) plain (all-purpose) flour + a little extra · 125 g (4 oz) butter · 3 egg yolks + 2 egg yolks, for coating · a pinch of salt · 1 tsp vanilla extract · 1 tbsp rum · 200 g (7 oz) ground hazelnuts · 110 g (3½ oz/generous ½ cup) brown sugar · 2 tbsp sour cream · ¼ tsp vanilla extract · ½ tsp zest of 1 lemon · 2 tbsp Amaretto or Grand Marnier

NUT CRESCENTS

Heat the milk and dissolve the yeast and sugar in it. Sieve the flour into a bowl, add the butter, egg yolks, salt, vanilla and rum, and knead into a smooth dough with the yeast and milk. Cover the mixture and let it rest for 45 minutes at room temperature.

Preheat the oven to 200°C (400°F/gas 6). Brown the hazelnuts in a pan until slightly toasted. Pour the sugar into 3 tablespoons of water and heat in a saucepan until the sugar has dissolved. Add the nuts, sour cream, vanilla, lemon zest and liqueur, and stir well. Boil for 10 minutes over a moderate heat, stirring occasionally. Leave to cool.

Briefly knead the dough, shape into a roll and cut into slices about 2 cm (¾ in) thick. Shape the dough slices into small balls on a work surface dusted with flour, then roll them into ovals. Take 1 tablespoon of the nut mixture, shape it into a roll, then lay it vertically on the oval of dough. Fold the dough over the nut mixture, creating a crescent-moon shape, then place on a baking parchment-lined baking (cookie) sheet. Whisk the egg yolks and coat each crescent with the beaten yolks. Leave to dry in a cool place for 1 hour. Preheat the oven to 200°C (400°F/gas 6), coat the crescents with a little more egg yolk and bake for about 20 minutes.

 MAKES 12–15

RUSSIA

AUSTRIA

GERMANY

INGREDIENTS

4 egg whites · a pinch of salt · 150 g (5 oz/⅔ cup) caster (superfine) sugar + 2 tbsp extra · 1 tsp vanilla extract · 150 g (5 oz/1¼ cups) plain (all-purpose) flour · ½ tsp ground cinnamon · 1 tbsp cocoa powder · 1 tbsp golden syrup or corn syrup

ALPHABET BISCUITS

Beat the egg whites with the salt until stiff. Gradually add the sugar and vanilla extract, then continue beating until firm and glossy. Mix the flour with the cinnamon and cocoa, and together with the syrup gradually blend into the beaten egg whites.

Preheat the oven to 160°C (320°F/gas 2). Fill the mixture into a piping bag with a small nozzle, and pipe letters onto baking (cookie) sheets lined with baking parchment. Bake in the oven for 10–15 minutes. Remove and leave to cool a little.

Meanwhile, for the glaze mix 2 tablespoons of sugar with 6 tablespoons of water and boil until the sugar has dissolved. Coat the letters with the glaze and leave to dry for a further 15 minutes in the switched-off oven.

Alphabet biscuits likely hail from St Petersburg, from where a Dresden 19th-century Vienna baker brought the recipe to Germany. Another legend has it that in 19th century Vienna Russian envoys were handed the biscuits by way of a greeting – a sort of Russian custom.

MAKES ABOUT 80

INDEX

Published in 2020 by Hardie Grant Books,
an imprint of Hardie Grant Publishing

Hardie Grant Books (London)
5th & 6th Floors
52–54 Southwark Street
London SE1 1UN

Hardie Grant Books (Melbourne)
Building 1, 658 Church Street
Richmond, Victoria 3121

hardiegrantbooks.com

Original edition © 2017 Hölker Verlag in der Coppenrath Verlag GmbH & Co. KG,
Hafenweg 30, 48155 Münster, Germany. Original title: Let it Snow: 24 Plätzchen und
Kekse für dich (ISBN 978-3-88117-145-8)

British Library Cataloguing-in-Publication Data. A catalogue record for this book
is available from the British Library.

Joy to the World
ISBN: 978-1-78488-373-7

10 9 8 7 6 5 4 3 2 1

For the German edition:
Photographer: Frauke Antholz
Editor: Jasmin Parapatits
Design: Katharina Khoss
Typesetting and lithography: Stefanie Bartsch

For the English edition:
Publishing Director: Kate Pollard
Editorial Assistant: Alexandra Lidgerwood
Translator: William Sleath
Typesetter: David Meikle
Cover design: Sophie Yamamoto
Proofreader: Kay Delves
Cover retoucher: Butterfly Creative Services

Colour reproduction by p2d
Printed and bound in China by Leo Paper Products Ltd.